Francis Frith's

Fifties Britain
Post-War Life

for

Thomas Lewys Perryman

In the hope that he will never again have to complain
when I say, 'In my day . . . .'
Diolch, cariad.

Francis Frith's
Fifties Britain
Post-War Life

Nigel Perryman

First published in the United Kingdom in 2002 by
The Francis Frith Collection

This edition published in 2012 by Bounty Books,
a division of Octopus Publishing Group,
Endeavour House, 189 Shaftesbury Avenue, London, WC2H 8JY, England

ISBN: 978-0-753723-70-8

British Library Cataloguing in Publication Data

Fifties Britain: Post-War Life
Nigel Perryman

The Francis Frith Collection
Oakley Business Park, Wylye Road,
Dinton, Wiltshire SP3 5EU
Tel: +44 (0) 1722 716 376
Email: info@francisfrith.co.uk
www.francisfrith.com

Printed and bound in China

Front Cover: HUNSTANTON, Fun Fair c1955 H135117p
The colour-tinting is for illustrative purposes only, and is not intended to be historically accurate

Every attempt has been made to contact copyright holders of illustrative material.
We will be happy to give full acknowledgement in future editions for any items not credited.
Any information should be directed to The Francis Frith Collection.

As with any historical database the Frith Archive is constantly being corrected and improved
and the publishers would welcome information on omissions or inaccuracies.

Wakefield, Wood Street W464005

B ritain never was a picture-postcard land of bucolic charms, of warm beer and cricket on the village green. But before World War II life was certainly comfortable for the majority: Britain still had its Empire; it was one of the richest countries in the world; living standards were rising; and even lower middle-class families had a maid of all work — known, sadly, as a 'slavey'.

Unfortunately there was a large minority of people who did not share in this prosperity, because they had no jobs. The unemployment statistics still horrify today: one in seven manual workers (75 percent of the working population) were unemployed on an average day; in the early 30s the figure was one in five. Even those who had relatively well-paid jobs had little job security and could lose everything, almost overnight — as happened to Lord Tebbit's father, who, famously, was forced to get on his bike to find work.

Sacrifice and change

Without the protection of a welfare state, the unemployed became trapped in a grim cycle of poverty and deprivation. Their diet consisted mainly of tea, bread, margarine, potatoes, stew and an occasional piece of bacon. By 1939, only 10 percent of Middlesborough's houses contained a bath and 35 percent had no electricity. Healthcare was paid for by insurance policies, which the poor could not afford, so few bothered with fripperies such as dentistry or spectacles. Secondary education cost money, too, so poor children could not break out of the cycle.

But the world was about to turn upside down — and Britain with it. War brought not only destruction and sacrifice but an opportunity for change. It was grasped eagerly, and by Queen Elizabeth II's Coronation, in June 1953, brave new Britain was ready to celebrate *(left),* sure that life would never be as harsh again.

'A good war'

World War II was not only generally regarded as a just war but as 'a good war', in historian AJP Taylor's phrase: 'good' because the economic controls needed to wage war established the basis of a new social order.

The principal catalyst for change was the disaster of Dunkirk, in June 1940, when the British Expeditionary Force was evacuated from France. As the author and journalist George Orwell reported, there was a general realisation of the 'utter rottenness' of the status quo.

Churchill's new Coalition Government, which had taken power the previous month, started to act. Ernest Bevin, previously the general secretary of a trade union but now the Minister for Labour,

assumed almost dictatorial powers. Soon there were 3.5 million men and women in uniform and 7.5 million women had been conscripted into the workforce, often doing jobs that had traditionally been the male preserve. By June 1944, only 54,000 were unemployed and average earnings had increased by 80 percent.

From cradle to grave

The general consensus was that the common interest and united endeavour of wartime Britain should be carried forward into the peace. Planning for brave new Britain had started as early as 1942, and in December of that year Sir William Beveridge published *Social Insurance and Allied Services,* championing full employment, a national

Guildford, High Street SG65002

Bournemouth, The Arcade B163153

health service and a safety net of social insurance to give security from 'the cradle to the grave.' Public approval was almost overwhelming.

The Labour Party endorsed the Beveridge Report wholeheartedly. Its manifesto for the 1945 election was titled *Let Us Face the Future*, and Michael Foot, a future Labour leader, summed it up: 'We shall not have won the peace until . . . every citizen . . . has a roof over his head, the chance to marry and bring up his children, safe from the fear of unemployment, sickness and war.' Labour won the election by a landslide, Churchill was ousted and it was time to win the peace.

The new Elizabethan age

The new government started briskly. In 1946 alone, the National Health Service was created, the coal industry and the railways were nationalised and the National Insurance Act was passed. But recurrent financial crises meant that austerity and even further rationing were still the order of the day.

By 1951, the government seemed exhausted and the hard times were becoming increasingly tiresome. 'Set the people free', said the Conservatives, and the people agreed — within a few years, rationing had been phased out.

Now there was a spring in Britain's stride. And when Mount Everest was conquered just before the Coronation ('All This — And Everest, Too,' trumpeted the *Daily Express*) brave new Britain seemed on top of the world. People spoke of the start of a new Elizabethan age of prosperity and success. And by 1957, Prime Minister Harold Macmillan could truthfully say: 'Most of our people have never had it so good.'

Uttoxeter, High Street U29005

In February 1947, designer Christian Dior launched his new fashion collection in Paris. He named it 'Corolla', after the whorl of petals inside a flower. 'We were emerging from a period of war, of uniforms, of women built like boxers,' he explained. 'I drew women-flowers, soft shoulders, flowering busts, fine waists like liana [vines] and wide skirts like corolla.' The women of a war ravaged world were quick to welcome his vision of softness and femininity but rejected his botanical imagery — they called it the 'New Look'.

It was particularly appealing to the women of drab, uniform and austere post-war Britain, but it was only practical for a privileged few. The New Look's long skirts demanded far more fabric than war-time 'utility' clothes, yet fabric was rationed until 1952. The body-shape was artificial, too, and depended on tight, waist-nipping corsetry and hip pads — which required even more fabric.

Adapt and change

Most women made do as best they could. Elements of the New Look, such as shirtwaists and full skirts, were adapted and became fashion staples for a decade, but the military influence was still very much apparent, with uniform-like suits and wide shoulders. For many men, though, fashion was hardly a consideration. They continued to dress as their fathers had done and as their sons would also do for some years yet.

Nevertheless, the world was changing. Having become used to working and enjoying a measure of financial independence during the War, women were reluctant to return to a purely domestic life, and the rise of consumerism made it hard for them to do so. So women strode out confidently in brave new Britain, as in this 1955 street scene in Uttoxeter, Staffordshire. And for an older generation of men it seemed as if the world had been turned upside down.

March, Broad Street M28010

There was nothing frivolous about fashion during World War II. Fabrics and the people who worked with them were both diverted to the war effort, and clothes rationing started in June 1941.

By 1945, British women had to cope with just 36 ration coupons a year: shoes needed seven (only five for wooden soles); a tweed suit took eighteen; and a blouse used up five. Utility regulations dictated the height of heels (no more than 2"), the amount of fabric in any outfit and the number of buttons and pleats. And the rules were strictly enforced: in 1947, Princess Elizabeth only received 100 extra coupons with which to dress for her marriage to the future Duke of Edinburgh.

The Utility collection

Determined to make the best of it, designers such as Hardy Amies and Norman Hartnell joined forces in the Incorporated Society of London Fashion Designers in 1942, and produced the Utility collection, which combined economy and style. It dominated day-to-day fashion for the average woman until the Utility regulations were abolished in March 1952.

Utility clothing for women meant wide, padded shoulders, a narrow waist, knee-length skirts in single colours, low heels and constant mending and making do. It also meant using Cyclax Stocking-less Cream and drawing seams on with an eyebrow pencil instead of nylon or silk stockings (unless you had a GI admirer). So it's hardly surprising that when restrictions started to ease women experimented with patterns and colours and the basics of the New Look *(left)*.

Demob

By August 1945, 171,000 men were being discharged from the services each month, and each one received the ubiquitous male uniform for Civvy Street: a high-waisted suit, a shirt, two separate collars, two pairs of socks, a pair of shoes, cufflinks, a tie and a hat.

Southend-on-Sea, the Golden Hind S155040

Dartford, Crown and Anchor Inn D3069

But men, too, soon started to rebel against pre-war standards. Lapels started to become wider and waists lower. Pleats and cuffs reappeared, and men started to appear in public without hats or ties *(far left)*.

Rock and roll is here to stay

Younger women, who had known nothing else, wanted to forget about austerity as soon as possible. The Italian designer Ferragamo helped: he perfected a steel support for heels, and stilettos become the rage. Then the wider availability of synthetic materials made it possible to emphasise hips and fill out skirts with layers of nylon frills *(left)*, often stiffened with a sugar solution. And then came rock and roll, to give them an opportunity to show off the results.

On April 12, 1954, 29-year-old Bill Haley and his Comets recorded *Rock Around the Clock*. Mothers and fathers couldn't understand what was going on — and that was the point.

Grays, the High Street G85015

Catalina.

Before World War II, people were expected to dress according to their position in life: the bank manager in his morning coat; the mother in her pinafore; the working man in his suit, tie and blue collar. And children and young people were meant to be seen but not heard. These expectations faded during the 50s. The country believed that it had fought to change the old ways, not preserve them — as it had proved by voting out Winston Churchill and electing a Labour government by a landslide in 1945.

Fashion, as always, reflected this. A new confidence and vibrancy were in the air and a new generation responded to that — even if some disapproved (above and above right).

Back to the one-piece

The two-piece bathing suit was created during the War to save fabric. Even so, much more fabric

Worthing, Beach Park W147024

Mevagissey, Bathing Girl M68114

was used than in the bikini, designed in 1946 and named after the US H-bomb tests on the Pacific island of Bikini Atoll. But after the War, when femininity was at a premium, women went back to the one-piece and flatteringly stretchy new synthetics.

There weren't any teenagers in post-war Britain: they hadn't been invented. Boys started their schooldays in shorts *(far right)* and only graduated to long trousers, in a rite of passage, when they went to secondary school — and sometimes not even then. As they grew older, they were expected to dress like their fathers, in regulation suits, though ties were not always insisted on and jumpers were permitted *(right)*. Girls were allowed a brief interim period of glamour before they married and settled down to a life of cosy motherhood and domesticity, untroubled by dreams of high living and *haute couture*.

Enter the bobby soxers

But things were about to change. In America, teenage girls cried over Frank Sinatra, the 'Sultan of Swoon'. These were the bobby soxers, with their penny loafers, sweaters, pleated skirts and Alice bands over tied-back hair. The writing was on the wall, and the fashion industry, among

Kinver, High Street K37045

Emsworth, South Street E62032

others, soon started to realise that young people had enormous potential spending power. Increasingly, music, clothes and films were targeted at them: *Rebel Without a Cause*, for example, starring James Dean who died in a car crash in 1955, and Marlon Brando's *The Wild One*, of 1953.

Coffee bars and beatniks

There was an alternative to this American world of motor bikes, fast cars and aggressive rebellion. Its influences were European

Biddulph B611015x

in the main, and it was a world of sleek Lambretta and Vespa scooters (with the girls — on the pillion, of course — wearing pedal pushers or shorts); of cappucinos and cool; of jazz, skiffle and existentialism. Gamine haircuts, cinched waists, Sloppy Joe sweaters and black leotards were the vogue, and sometimes feet were even bare *(far left)*.

There's nothing so cruel . . .

Teenagers and beatniks there may have been, but kids would still be kids. The theory had it that the class system was breaking down, but the practice was that the prejudices of generations could not be abandoned so quickly. And, as always, fashion pointed up the class distinctions.

As this photograph *(above)* shows, a boy who wore a tie, had pulled-up socks, shined shoes, a smart haircut and a buttoned-up jacket walked some streets at his peril. And yet . . . there's a certain provocative superciliousness about his bearing. The older boys seem to have seen it all before and are just waiting in the doorway, mildly interested to see what happens next.

Nowadays we tend to dress down for a day at the seaside: in blouses, T-shirts and jeans; flip-flops and deck shoes. But when young Eastenders went on a Sunday outing in brave new Britain — surprisingly, here, to Folkestone rather than Southend — they very definitely dressed up. Floral prints and bright patterns were ideal for the summer and were teamed with large woven straw

Folkestone, Cockles and Whelks F35154

clutch bags. And in those days white stilettos spoke of elegance and style rather than Essex.

Men dressed sharply, too. Jackets had become longer, shoulders were less padded and lapels had become slimmer. A suit was still the prerequisite of formality, but it could be set off by a nonchalant slouch and greased, coiffed hair. And after the jellied eels? A nice cup of tea.

Bournemouth B163079x

Polruan, Fore Street P69043

Leatherhead, High Street L26040

Folkestone, the Quayside F35152a

In 1944, R A B Butler's Education Act became law, and working class children were given the opportunity to go to grammar schools. It marked a sea change in society as well as in education.

By the mid-50s, many of these children had left the new universities to become 'Angry Young Men'. Society may have expected their gratitude, but instead it received their contempt. Like Jimmy Porter in John Osborne's *Look Back in Anger*, first performed in April 1956, they railed against what they saw as the stifling social conventions of the day. The result was a generation that dared to hold hands in public, wear dark glasses and dress casually *(top and above, right)*. Conventional, smartly suited, hatted pillars of society *(above, left)* duly took offence.

Despite the challenges that the conventions faced from Angry Young Men, rock and rollers and beatniks, each in their own ways, some sections of society clung like limpets to their traditions. Often these seemed frozen in an Edwardian time warp, in an age when the sun never set on the British Empire and Prime Minister Harold Macmillan's 'winds of change' had not even started to rustle in Africa.

Clinging on

These day trippers to Holy Island *(below),* off Northumberland's coast, look for all the world like members of a house party after World War I rather than World War II. Hats are *de rigeur*, even for children.But while captain and crewman wear practical, sturdy sweaters and trousers, suited to their task, the trippers are constrained in formal suits and ties, and, in the case of the lady, a long, flowing dress that hardly seems an appropriate outfit for choppy coastal waters. (Wearing plus-fours releases the gentleman in the middle from his obligation to wear either a tie or a hat.) The class division could not be more clear.

Perhaps the unchanging world of the Island's Lindisfarne Monastery reassured them — some things, after all, were set in stone — and made it easier to raise a smile for the camera.

Holy Island, Fashion H348133x

Burry Port, Station Road B472059

Despite the recalcitrance of the few, brave new Britain had changed out of all recognition by the end of the 50s. And the country was on the cusp of an even greater social revolution, which was to lead to the 'Swinging Sixties' and usher in the age of Prime Minister Harold Wilson's 'white heat of technology' — and also of the pill, the permissive society, the Beatles and flower power.

Grown-ups still dressed with conspicuous formality, for work and social functions at least. But among Britain's youth — the next working generation — respect for both social and sartorial conventions had eroded to such an extent that a critical mass of disregard had built up. It first became unstable, and then unstoppable.

Relaxed confidence

The evidence for this wasn't hard for Francis Frith's photographers to find. Even in Burry Port,

a sleepy harbour in West Wales, two young men stand confidently, even cockily, by their pride and joy, a waxed and polished Vauxhall Victor — very much that year's model — wearing clothes and demonstrating an attitude that might well have caused a riot ten years earlier.

The man on the left sports a Tony Curtis quiff and a white T-shirt (T-shirts had been introduced to Britain as part of American GI uniform during World War II, and were later popularised on screen by Marlon Brando and James Dean). His friend, equally relaxed, wears a low-buttoned cardigan of the type favoured by angry young intellectuals and the coffee bar set.

Nice girls wear skirts?

Young women's fashions, of course, also reflected and pointed up the mood of the times. In the seaside resort of Clovelly, Devon, a young woman wears trousers *(right)* — to what appears to be the surprise of an older woman outside the shop. Women had worn trousers during the War, and after it, but until the late 60s they were not considered quite respectable; many executives insisted that their secretaries wore skirts rather than trousers in the office.

Meanwhile, in respectable Poole, Dorset, young women were wearing not only short shorts, but flip-flops. Norman Hartnell, Christian Dior and the like would have been horrified, but this was how the new Britain was shaping. And the proverbial man on the Clapham omnibus was probably thinking, 'What next? Long hair on men?'

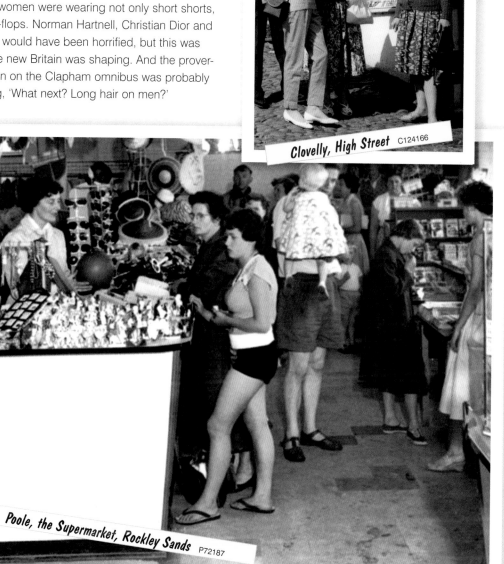

Clovelly, High Street C124166

Poole, the Supermarket, Rockley Sands P72187

Luton, Conveyor Belt, Vauxhall Motors L117046

In August 1945, J L Hodson, a journalist, wrote in his diary: 'The war is over; the conditions of war in some respect continue . . . A journey which in peacetime took four hours now took eight-and-a-quarter. No food on the train. No cup of tea to be got at the stops . . . no taxi to be got.' Motoring conditions were equally tiresome, even though the wartime blackout had been lifted. The road network was only adequate for local rather than national travel — it could take a whole day to drive from London to Edinburgh — and petrol was still rationed. There were only about two million private cars in Britain, however, so while the roads were bad they were also empty, and driving could

All change

It was obvious that something had to be done. Britain could hardly develop a thriving post-war economy without a transport system that functioned adequately. It was vital that the nation got on the move again.

The Labour government's manifesto in its successful 1945 election campaign had been called 'Let's Face the Future', and it advocated public ownership, a planned economy and social reform. Change was not slow to come. In January 1946, test flights started at Heathrow airport, where a 3,000-yard runway was flanked by a row of huts and tents; and on December 16, a £20 million expansion plan was announced.

Two days later, on December 18, Labour MPs sang *The Red Flag* in triumph as the House of Commons voted to nationalise the railways, road haulage and the ports. The Conservatives claimed that disaster was inevitable, but the public seemed to approve. At the time, that is, because by 1950 only 30 percent of those polled by Gallup thought that the nationalisation of the railways had been a 'good thing'.

The open road

Soon cars rather than tanks started to roll off the production lines, among them the Velox *(left)* from the Vauxhall works in Luton, Bedfordshire, in 1950. It was hard going for the car manufacturers, however, because a steel shortage in 1951 brought the production lines to a halt (a coal shortage also cut train services).

Even so, by 1955 there were more than 3.8 million cars on the roads. A few years later, they could be driven on Britain's first stretch of motorway — as was Prime Minister Harold Macmillan, who opened the eight-mile Preston bypass on December 5, 1958. And Vauxhall's Luton works continued to thrive, until, ironically, it produced its last car in 2002, Queen Elizabeth II's Jubilee Year.

still be a pleasure — unconstrained by parking tickets, breathalysers, seat belts, MOTs or any speed restrictions (let alone speed cameras) apart from a 30mph limit in built-up areas.

But for the vast majority, trains, buses, trolleybuses, trams, bicycles or motorbikes were the only means of getting around.

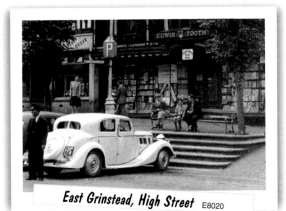

East Grinstead, High Street E8020

What drove the demand for cars — there were more than nine million of them by the mid-60s — was not just convenience but a desire for status. This desire, in its turn, was driven by the advertising industry, which discovered after the war that consumer goods could be sold by linking brand images to a desirable lifestyle.

General Motors, in America, led the trend. As its president, Charles E Wilson, maintained, what was good for General Motors was good for the country — and that meant selling more cars to help fuel the expanding economy. So a Buick made you 'Feel the man you are', while a Cadillac

Newport Pagnell, Swan Hotel N62043

Washington W359005

was 'flashy' and a Mercury was 'assertive and modern'. The US car industry revelled in excessive consumption, of fuel and chrome alike, with cars becoming ever longer, lower, and flashier.

Chrome at a premium

In Britain, car lovers could only look on and dream, perhaps of importing a gleaming American automobile sleek with chrome *(left, top)*. Shortages of materials, and, perhaps, a certain inbuilt reticence, meant that the new family car was more likely to be a black four-door saloon *(below)*, boasting eight horsepower, a starter

motor and orange, flick-out semaphore indicators. The car would be washed, polished and buffed on a Sunday morning. The models introduced later were less sedate, but hardly American in style: the Austin A35 *(left, bottom)*, for example, or the Ford Popular, introduced in September 1953 at a cost of £390, including tax.

On the never never

Before 1958, when hire purchase restrictions were eventually abolished, few could afford £390. So the majority still relied on bicycles *(below)*, buses and trains *(over)*.

Huntingdon, High Street H136002

Barnsley, the Bus Station B333037

Bournemouth, Richmond Hill B163025

Buses were one of the success stories of post-war Britain. They gradually started to take the place of trams and trolley-buses *(above)*, while the numbers of rail passengers remained more or less static. By 1952, buses and coaches accounted for about 75 percent of total mileage travelled, an increase of one-and-a-half times since 1938.

These statistics may be dull, but there is a story behind them. A bus is versatile: it does not need an infrastructure of overhead cables or tramlines. It is not confined to large cities, but can take children to school, people to work or shoppers to the high street *(right)*. It can also link to other forms of transport: to a railway terminus *(previous pages)* or to cars *(above, right)*. And what could be more pleasant than lazing down country lanes to Lorna Doone's farm *(over)* on a sunny afternoon?

Above all, though, buses were one of the few forms of classless transport in post-war Britain. Cars were for officialdom and the well-off, and third class was not abolished on the railways until June 1956. Very much in the spirit of the times, buses were practical, friendly and unstuffy. Any more fares please?

January 1 1954

Flashing indicator lights become legal on UK cars.

Grt London, Chessington, Car Park   C221018

Truro, Boscowen Street   T86021

Guildford, High Street G65003

The towns of post-war Britain were fairly peaceful. The odd car might disturb this peace, as might the clip-clop of a horse's hooves, because a horse and cart was still far from an uncommon sight. Parking was freely available and it was neither too difficult nor too dangerous to cross the road. But this relative tranquillity was soon to be shattered, not only by the increasing number of cars but by the sheer bustle of brave new Britain.

Sir Leslie (later Lord) Hore-Belisha, the Minister for Transport, had foreseen the future in 1934. He devised the 'Belisha beacon' *(above)*. Taller than head-high, it was a yellow, glass beacon on a striped pole that marked a place, delineated by studs on the road, at which it was safe to cross — assuming that due care was taken. Certainly, a degree of caution was necessary, because drivers tended to ignore the beacons.

For this reason, zebra crossings, with black and white stripes painted on the road, were introduced in 1951 (the stripes were going to be red and white, but it was decided that they would be too intrusive). Any pedestrian who placed a foot on a zebra crossing was deemed to have precedence over a car. Success was not immediate, however. In December 1951, one in five respondents to a Gallup poll felt that they were unsafe to use; by June 1954, three out of ten still agreed.

The urban landscape changes
Belisha beacons, zebra crossings and what later came to be called 'traffic pollution' changed the landscape of urban Britain. Parking became a major problem *(below, right)*, and much as drivers argued against them, regulations to control parking became inevitable.

Nevertheless, it took time before they came into force. Double-yellow parking lines were first seen in London in June 1958, and the next month parking meters appeared in London's Mayfair.

But motoring was still an almost carefree pursuit in those halcyon days. Too much so, some thought: in a 1955 Gallup poll, three out of five drivers believed that everyone should have to retake a driving test every few years. And a 1957 poll discovered, unsurprisingly, that one in two men thought that men were better drivers than women; surprisingly, one in five women agreed.

And the country's, too

It wasn't only Britain's towns that were changing. More cars needed more petrol, and as 'going out for a drive' became a favourite recreation, garages sprang up like weeds throughout the countryside *(right)*.

Fair Oak, the Village F164016

Leighton Buzzard, High Street L211028

Silecroft, the Railway Station S657018

Trains and boats and planes

'Rumbling under blackened girder, Midland,
bound for Cricklewood,
Puffed its sulphur to the sunset where the Land
of Laundries stood.
Rumble under, thunder over, train and tram
alternate go.'

John Betjeman's romantic view of the railways, from *Parliament Hill Fields*, wasn't shared by everyone. Steam trains may have looked attractive *(above)*, but most people, who had to endure cramped third-class carriages, found them crowded, dirty, smelly and slow. They cheered when the government announced a £1,240 million electrification programme in 1955.

Meanwhile, people increasingly abandoned the railways and drove, even if they sometimes had to use a slightly racketty-looking ferry *(right, below)*. And the aviation industry *(above, right)* was opening up even more enticing possibilities.

Clacton-on-Sea, the Airfield C107079

January 25, 1955
The government announces
a £1,240-million plan
to electrify the railways.

Torpoint, Ferry T63002

Newport Pagnell, M1 Motorway N62057

Lydd, Ferryfield Airport L333030

Euxton, M6 Motorway from Runshaw Lane E207014

By the end of the 50s, brave new Britain was truly on the move. On November 9, 1959, the first stretch of the M1 was opened. Many people found it something of a culture shock: the six glistening lanes of asphalt were viewed as a tourist attraction, and on the Sunday after the opening crowds of sightseers flocked to admire them — some even picnicked on the approach roads.

Traffic was light at first, though new motorway police units *(above)* kept a wary eye on smart cars — here a Ford Zodiac — that looked as if they might break the speed limits.

Up and away

It was not just motor transport that was taking a quantum leap into the future. A different route to a whole new world of overseas leisure was being opened up by air travel. The first company in the market was Silver City Airways *(left)*, which used ex-World War II transport aircraft. Starting in 1948, it carried cars from Lympne, in Kent, to Le Touquet in France. For those who could afford it, the trip was a revelation that opened up new vistas of sophisticated European living. The classic newspaper headline, 'Fog in the Channel — Continent cut off', started to seem just a little parochial.

And it didn't end there. The first passenger jet to cross the Atlantic took off in 1958, and a year later the first package holidays to Spain were offered to the public: 15 days in Majorca for 44 guineas. By 1960, 3.5 million Britons had been abroad. And they still hadn't invented Club 18-30.

Corringham, Woodbrook Way C243046

Bombs destroyed around six-and-a-half percent of Britain's homes during the War, and damaged many more. London's Blitz, the raid on Coventry and the attacks on south-east England (known as 'Hellfire Corner') are well-remembered; less so is the fact that most of the country's major cities and ports also suffered. In Hull, for example, 7,444 homes were destroyed and 86,722 damaged.

Many of the homes that did survive the War were scarcely fit for the return of conquering heroes. A 1930s slum-clearance programme had been interrupted by the conflict, leaving around a million families living in squalor. Even those in better accommodation endured living conditions that were far from ideal in brave new Britain: without hot running water, kettles were boiled on the stove to fill a galvanised zinc tub in front of the fire for the weekly bath; often the lavatory was a privy at the bottom of the garden; and in many families all the children had to share a bed.

Home, sweet home

As with transport, something had to be done. In fact, 41 percent of the electorate considered housing to be the main issue of the day.

What lay behind this was partly a feeling that the hard work and sacrifices that had brought about victory should be rewarded, and partly sheer practicality. The post-war 'baby boom' was under way — the number of births increased by a third — and more living space was needed desperately. As many as four million more homes were thought to be needed within ten years.

But there was also the idea of 'bettering yourself', which pervaded post-war society. Everyman's dream (and Everywoman's, too) was to swap an inner-city terrace house for a three-bedroom, centrally heated detached Dunroamin, as in Woodbrook Way, Corringham, Essex *(left)* — preferably with a shiny new car parked outside.

Essex, Jaywick, "B" Type Bungalow J4026

The need for housing was so immediate that the repair of 125,000 bomb-damaged houses could not satisfy it. But then someone — it's not clear who — had a brainwave. Aircraft factories were stuffed with supplies of aluminium and steel and had the technicians to work with these materials: instead of making planes, they could build prefabricated houses.

And so prefabs were born. Aluminium sections no more than 7' 6" wide (the maximum width permitted for road transport) were taken to the site by lorry and assembled there, often by prisoners of war, in just three days. The idea proved so successful that 125,000 were ordered straightaway.

'Palaces for the people'

Today only a few aficionados champion prefabs; most of us think of them as shabby and decaying. But in their day, prefabs were extremely popular — they were nicknamed 'palaces for the people'.

South Ockendon, Celandine Road S280010

Lewes, Prefabs in Lanport L40028a

DAILY MAIL BOOK OF
HOUSE PLANS
1956

NEW DESIGNS—INCLUDING EXHIBITS AT THE
DAILY MAIL IDEAL HOME EXHIBITION 1956

2'6

It's not hard to see why. Each prefab sat proud and detached in an area of garden *(left and above)*. It had a modern kitchen, with metal, wipe-clean surfaces, a gas cooker and — almost unheard of in those days — a gas fridge. There was hot running water, too, and a modern bathroom with a basin, bath and lavatory. It was all a far cry from zinc tubs and outside privies.

In time, other designs superseded that of the prefab, such as the B-type bungalow *(left, above)*. Prefabs were only intended to last for ten years, after all. But they are still with us today, and they may be with us for a long time yet: in October 2001 it was announced that 20 prefabs in Bristol were being considered for listed building status.

Heybridge H174022

Most of the new homes were built on greenfield sites, allowing each family not only a sense of community but also personal space and privacy — a luxury at the time, but one that was much sought after by young couples who had been forced by necessity to start married life living with one or other set of parents. These timber-framed bungalows *(above),* guarded by well-tended privet hedges, stand quietly proud, satisfied and confident: a solid, understated expression of the certainty that every Englishman's home is his castle. (In fact, the castles may not have been quite so English, because Sweden sent Britain a goodwill consignment of timber to help meet the demand for new homes.)

A secret garden
This extra living space, together with ease of access to the countryside — Pitsea *(above right)* was a rural community before being absorbed into the new town of Basildon — was a delight

for the baby boomer children. Beforehand they had been forced to play on inner-city streets, or in playgrounds tacked on to estate developments *(right, below).* Now they could play in gardens and leafy avenues, generally undisturbed by the presence of cars, explore verdant wildernesses, fish for sticklebacks in a meandering stream or go blackberrying.

Such fun!
And what a time they had. There were street games, such as chain tag, British bulldog and hopscotch. More irritatingly, there was also 'ginger knocking': children who had read too many *Just William* books tied long pieces of string to doorbells, hid around a corner and ran away giggling when a door was answered. And the *sine qua non* for every child was a go-cart, made of planks of wood, fitted with old pram wheels and steered by reins of string. There may have been tears by bedtime, but it was such fun.

February 3, 1955

The government announces that a record 347,605 new homes were built during 1954.

Pitsea P145011

Aveley, Children's Corner A110009

Killamarsh, Rectory Road K116021

By the mid-50s, new housing tended to be concentrated on estates *(above)*. There was little sense of leafy, tree-lined suburbia, more of no-nonsense, semi-detached practicality. Partly this was because of cost: housing subsidies had been reduced, and the cost of labour had risen along with social expectations.

There was also a general desire to own one's own home rather than rent it. In the early 50s it had cost 15 shillings a week to rent a pre-fab, but by 1957 the average price of a three-bedroomed house was £2,280 (the average wage was £9 14s 6d a week) and mortgages were hard to come by. So desires had to be tailored to means.

Style wars

These houses may look conformist, but inside them a style war was almost certainly raging.

October 26 1955
Housing subsidies are cut in the Autumn budget.

Before World War II, decor was based on shades of chocolate brown, bottle green and nicotine cream. But in brave new Britain, there was a move to airiness, lightness and vivid colours: tangerine, turquoise, aquamarine, lemon and apricot. Wallpaper was patterned, often with bright flowers, or even with plates and fruit for the kitchen.

Many households remained conservative, though. The focal point of the sitting room (called a 'lounge' by the upwardly mobile) was still the coal fire, with its accompanying coal scuttle and revolving set of fire irons, comprising poker, tongs and brush. A mirror would be positioned above the fireplace, and to its right would be a bakelite wireless. Mum and dad would have chairs by the fire — dressed, of course, with anti-macassars to guard against stains from men's Brylcreemed hair — and all would be right with the world.

East Dereham, Moorgate Estate D25022

January 16, 1958
Research reveals that cases of pre-war 'suburban neurosis' have been seen in the new housing estates.

One of the main protagonists in these style wars was TV's Mr DIY, Barry Bucknell. *Do It Yourself* (he practically invented the phrase), his television series, had an extraordinary influence on both home decor and marital harmony. His programme went out live, so all his mishaps were laid bare to an avid public; and they were mirrored by the scenes of domestic discord that followed his assurances that anybody could transform their home given a few tools, a little formica and the desire to do so.

Chrome and formica

Soon, though house exteriors may all have appeared uniform, as on these pages, their interiors become a celebration of individualism — depending, of course, on the skill of the DIY-er involved. Here there might be a telephone table with a padded seat; there a cocktail bar, glorying in chrome and padded stools.

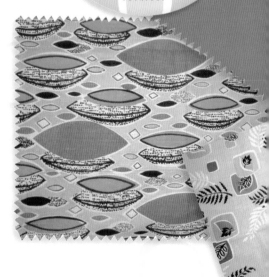

Almost universally, though, door panels, fireplaces and any other period features were ripped out and covered with hardboard and formica, while stacked occasional tables became a must.

Design rules

Interior design (a new concept) was also influenced by the establishment of the Design Council in 1956. By 1958, it had approved more than 8,000 items, including the G-plan range of stylish, lightweight furniture. The time was coming closer when a British home could look like something out of *I Love Lucy*.

Calne, Newcroft Road C228083

Herne Hill, Dorchester Court H410010

Stevenage, Bedwell Park S191069

The most significant contribution to resolving post-war Britain's housing problems came with the creation of the new towns. In 1946, Lewis Silkin, Minister of Town and Country Planning, presented the New Towns Act. Fourteen of them were planned at first (later there would be 31): eight, including Hemel Hemstead and Stevenage, outside London's Green Belt; and six further afield, including Cwmbrân, in Wales, and East Kilbride, in Scotland.

A new Stevenage, to be built next to an existing community, was designated as Britain's first new town on November 11, 1946. Then, Old Stevenage's population was 6,450: the new town was planned to house 60,000 in 20 years, as Londoners were relocated and their families grew. This was not natural growth, but an experiment in social engineering — almost Stalinist, some thought. One wag put up a sign labelling

Stevenage's railway station 'Silkingrad'. And when a 1948 Gallup poll asked people to comment on the government's proposal to take over all the pubs in the new towns, 49 percent disapproved — socialism, they may have thought, could only be taken so far.

Spend, spend, spend!

Nevertheless, the new Stevenage was a success, by and large. It was certainly up-to-the-minute, at the cutting edge of town planning. Bedwell Park *(left, above)* was the first part of Stevenage New Town to be built: airy and open, with walkways and greenery designed to be integral to the whole concept, it was revolutionary.

So, too, were the facilities, which were very much attuned to the overwhelming consumerism that pervaded the 50s. Queensway *(below, left)*, the pedestrianised town centre, was the first traffic-free shopping zone in Britain. Queen Elizabeth II opened Queensway and unveiled panels on the Clock Tower *(below)* in 1959. Meanwhile, in the never-had-it-so-good late-50s, shoppers thronged to spend, spend, spend.

August, 1955
The shops sell out of women's skin-tight denim jeans.

Stevenage, Queensway S191095

Stevenage, the Town Square S191304

Hunstanton, Fun Fair H135117

Par Bay, the Beach P7049

Britain's beaches were closed during the war. Many of them had been laid with mines and criss-crossed by barbed wire, and buckets and spades, sandcastles, a paddle and a laze on the sand *(above)* were a distant memory by 1945. Instead, holidaymakers had to rely on seaside funfairs for their entertainment, with Coca-Cola (bottled in Britain since 1938), the intriguingly salacious pleasures of 'What the Butler Saw' machines and the usually unprofitable delights of one-armed bandits and penny-pushers, as in Hunstanton, Norfolk *(previous pages)*.

This was a considerable hardship because before the war a trip to the seaside had been by far the most popular means of getting away from it all: 20 million people were estimated to have visited the seaside during 1939. So when the army had removed the barbed wire and mines, and bulldozed the tank traps and pillboxes, people streamed back to the beaches and their traditional delights. This stream became a torrent after 1948, when the Holidays With Pay Act guaranteed workers two-weeks' paid holiday a year.

A family affair

Though the attractions of a seaside holiday had never been in doubt, they were even more appealing in brave new Britain. For years, families had been apart, and now they had the opportunity to rebuild family life. Mum, Dad and the extended family could get to know each other again.

As always, in Britain, the weather had a knack of putting a damper on proceedings. On a good day, you could run around and have a paddle *(below, right)*, or even go shrimping. Sometimes, though, there was nothing for it but to brace yourself against the stormy spray *(below, left)*, or to sit, stoically, through a drab day on a pebbled beach, determined at least to give the appearance of having a good time *(bottom)*. But there were always seashells to be gathered, to linger wistfully on the mantleshelf and bring back happy memories long after the journey home.

Trevose, Treyarnon Bay T78039

Westward Ho, High Seas W71071

1957
'Love Letters in the Sand' is the hit of the year.

Yarmouth, the Beach Y4012

Lowestoft, the Cliff Putting Green L105089

It wasn't just the prospect of lazy days on the beach that drew the crowds to Britain's holiday resorts, of course. There was just so much to do — almost too much, in fact.

After a leisurely beach picnic, or even a bag of chips and a cup of cockles, you could meander along to the municipal putting green *(above)* and play a round, doing everything possible to hide your competitive spirit but to win, nevertheless. (A tremendously popular book of the time was Stephen Potter's *The Theory and Practice of Gamesmanship, or the Art of Winning Games Without Actually Cheating,* published in 1947.)

Those less vigorously inclined could aid their digestion by taking a trip on a miniature railway *(right)*, which appealed equally to children, courting couples and the young at heart.

Wish you were here

Other distractions for the children included sailing model yachts and taking a donkey ride *(far right)*. For young people, the purchase of a Kiss-me-Kwik hat was almost obligatory, while the whole family signed a seaside postcard for friends back home saying, inevitably, 'Wish you were here'.

Lowestoft, the Pier, the Miniature Railway L105076

Lowestoft, Punch and Judy Children's Corner L105079

The nation's favourite postcards were drawn by Donald McGill, who specialised in depicting well-rounded women and hen-pecked husbands. 'Some people come down here for a holiday and some bring their wives with them,' was the caption to one favourite.

But McGill's cards were often saucy, too. So much so that in 1954 Grimsby's humourless council officials banned them. They were shocked, for example, by his card showing a man asking a sales assistant in a newsagent's shop: 'Excuse me miss, do you keep stationery?' The blushing beauty's reply was: 'Well, sometimes I wiggle around a bit.' Unshocked, holidaymakers bought them by the million.

Blood and thunder

Another favourite, in the days long before political correctness, was a Punch and Judy show on the beach *(left)*, with much fun to be had as villainous Mr Punch beat his wife, among many others, while Toby, the dog, looked on. And then, time for tea at the guest-house, with fish-paste sandwiches, a nice slice of fruitcake and a snooze.

Lowestoft, Model Yacht Pond and Donkeys L105123

Lowestoft, South Pier L105100

Two more seaside holiday experiences were eagerly anticipated. The first, an excursion by boat *(right, above)* — usually either round the bay or to a nearby island to see either monks or bird colonies. The real pleasure here came from seeing who would become seasick: did little Johnny look queasy?; was Mum quite alright? The second experience was more anticipatory: would Dad remember how to put up a deckchair? *(right)*, or would he hurt his hands, become enveloped in canvas and lose his temper just like last year?

'Cross my palm with silver'

In the end, though, all roads in a seaside resort led to the pier *(above)*. A languid stroll along the esplanade was an experience in itself — all human life was there. And then there were the delights of the pier: toffee apples, end-of-pier shows, amusements arcades, souvenir shops and a mysterious gypsy who would tell you of a tall, dark, handsome stranger if you crossed her palm with silver.

July 7, 1945
A record 102,889 day-trippers travel by train to Blackpool to visit beaches newly reopened after the War.

Southend-on-Sea, the Beach S155004

Canvey Island, the Beach C237005

Mablethorpe, Donkey Rides M1053p

Nowadays it's very different. For the purposes of the Horses (Protective Headgear for Young Riders) Act, 1990, a donkey is a horse, so riding one without a protective helmet is an offence. But the regulations don't stop there. Donkey rides must be licenced, and each donkey must have a veterinary certificate, an identifying hoof brand and a designated rest day a week. All very proper, too — but perhaps it's no surprise that only around 850 donkeys work on Britain's beaches today.

Another age

Regulations were few and far between on the wind-swept Norfolk beach by Butlin's Filey Camp in the early 50s *(above)*. Both donkeys and children were less well-protected in those days, and youngsters were expected to put up with their share of bumps and bangs and bounce straight back.

For an urban generation a donkey ride was exciting, exhilarating and a little nerve-wracking, inspiring dreams at home and tales at school.

Skegness, Butlins Holiday Camp 147024

Ilkley, The Swimming Pool 16006

'Holiday with pay! Holiday with play! A week's holiday for a week's wage,' was Billy Butlin's slogan in 1934, when he announced his plans for Britain's first holiday camp (above and right, middle) — it opened two years later, in Skegness ('so bracing'). He offered three square meals a day and endless entertainments and activities for £3 a head, with no extra charges.

The Butlin's formula was an immediate success. Another camp was built at Clacton and camps at Filey, Pwllheli and Ayr followed just after the war. By 1948, one in twenty holidaymakers took their holidays at Butlin's.

'Good morning, campers'
Today, the idea of spending a holiday at a post-war Butlin's is far from attractive — indeed, the original formula had started to lose its appeal as early as the 60s. The chalets were arranged in straight lines, as if in a military camp and there were barbed-wire fences and communal bathrooms. Constant instructions blared out from the tannoy system: get up; queue for breakfast; go to the lido; buy an ice cream; don't forget the three-legged race — and so on, right through until bedtime. Even the camp in television's Hi-De-Hi was less regimented.

Are we happy? Yes we are!
Yet regimentation was familiar to the post-war generation, and Butlin's brought back happy memories of wartime camaraderie and a spirit of mucking in and making do. Besides, there was no argument about the advantages of a holiday camp.

An all-in fee meant that there were no strains on the budget, and, more importantly for many mothers, nannies looked after the children in the evening. So Mum and Dad could dance the night away, without a care in the world.

Butlin's

FOR YOUR HOLIDAY

where you make new friends . . . .

BUTLIN'S HOLIDAY CAMP, SKEGNESS

CARD
FOR ADDRESS ONLY

11 AUG
1952
LINCS.

Caister-on-Sea, Holiday Camp (Billiard Room)   C450050

A post-war Butlin's camp was like a small town — or, perhaps more accurately, a military base with all the necessary support facilities set in a fenced park. There was really very little reason for people to set foot outside the camp during their holiday, and many families never did.

Practically everything you could want was on-site: a shopping arcade, a hairdressing salon, a post office, a newsagent, a launderette and even a church.

Perpetual motion

There was always something to keep you occupied — and someone, too, because the ubiquitous 'Red Coats' stood ready to pounce on those who seemed to be slacking or not enjoying themselves enough and chivvy them into motion.

At Butlin's Filey Camp, for example, you could learn to master a bicycle built for rather more than two *(right)*, to the unconcealed admiration of the onlookers. Or you could have a go at roller skating *(below)*, while crowds watched to see if you fell over. Fairgrounds and boating lakes were always popular, while the swimming pool was often the focus of a camp's activities. Some camps even sported miniature railways, chairlifts, water-rides and monorails.

Caister-on-Sea, Holiday Camp Roller Skating Rink C450012

Caister-on-Sea, The Holiday Camp C450025

If you had the inclination and any energy left (and if you didn't, you wouldn't be fitting in and so would be 'too good for the likes of us') you could always enter the almost relentless procession of competitions. You could be judged to have the shiniest bald head, for example, or the knobbliest knees; or enter the sack race. For their part, young ladies could contest the bathing beauty competition in a swimsuit parade, or vie to win Lux soap's prize for the best complexion.

No rest for the wicked
There were further delights on offer in the evening: professional theatre shows, talent competitions, bars, dance halls, and housey housey. And so to bed — quite exhausted.

Worthing, the Paddling Pool W147028

Poole, The Boating Centre, Rockley Sands P72131

Butlin's soon had its imitators, but these were rarely a patch on the original. Often, entrepreneurs just bought up derelict military camps by the seaside and renovated them; the fictional camp in television's *Hi-De-Hi* is a classic example. The ethos was the same as that of Butlin's, but the facilities and professionalism lacked something by comparison. Nevertheless, near compulsory fun and games were still the order of the day *(far right, below)* — even if this King Neptune is a very long way from the equator!

Pockets of resistance

Even though the holiday camps went from strength to strength, many people proved resistant to their charms. The elderly, for example, still preferred to observe the pre-war tradition of a less frenetic holiday by the sea, with the opportunity for a gentle, though keenly fought, post-prandial game of bowls *(right)*.

Young children, too, still loved the sand and spume, the seashells, shrimps and sandcastles of a holiday by the sea, even if ever-watchful parents sometimes confined them to a more mundane municipal paddling pool *(above)*.

Clacton-on-Sea, The Bowling Green C107065

The middle classes, and of course, those aspiring to middle-class status in class-conscious, upwardly mobile brave new Britain, rejected all forms of regimentation — and, in particular, anything that might be thought of as 'non-U'. Butlin's was considered to almost embody the term.

Instead, they arranged their own holidays and their own diversions while away. Families might hire a holiday cottage in Dorset, say, and do a spot of dinghy sailing *(left)*. Or, to really impress the neighbours, they might take the car on a ferry to France, and experiment with frogs' legs, snails, garlic (too much for many people's taste) and paté — at the time, all were considered strange, exotic and a little un-British.

Cha-cha-change

Sadly, for the nostalgic, the attractions of both seaside holidays and holiday camps started to fade towards the end of the 50s. People wanted a break with the past, and the new package holiday firms were quick to offer it to them: sangria in Spain, rather than warm beer in Blackpool.

1948
The Holidays with Pay Act is passed, entitling every British worker to two weeks paid holiday.

Christchurch, Wick Ferry Holiday Camp C99150

Poole, Sunset on Bay Hollow, Rockley Sands P72122

For some, the crowds and regimentation of a holiday camp were anathema, as was the hustle and bustle of a seaside resort. They preferred to take to the open road, to travel at their own pace and choose their own destinations.

Before the war, caravanning had been associated with the well-to-do, the only people who could afford cars. But as car ownership spread through society, a caravan holiday became a practical possibility for many more. Caravans became more affordable, too, particularly as the first post-war models, such as the 1946 Eccles 'Enterprise', were built on strictly utilitarian lines. Later, caravans became more sleek and almost luxurious — for example the popular 'Sprite', of 1954.

Rural delights
One problem in the early days was that the few caravan sites that were available were so packed that they resembled holiday camps *(above, and right, below)* and they hardly reflected the freedom and spontaneity that caravanning was meant to be all about.

Donald Chidson, of the Caravan Club, provided another option with his successful campaign to establish small, more intimate caravan sites on farms *(right, above),* where you could take your ease more privately.

Bognor Regis, Lidsey Camp B130135

Rossall, Ockwells Caravan Camp R409009

Beaconsfield, Model Village   B609066

There wasn't much time for recreation during the war. And even if you had the time, there was rarely very much to do. Tourist attractions were stripped of staff, zoos and fairgrounds were closed and posters sternly asked the question 'Is your journey really necessary?' to discourage you from using valuable fuel on a day trip in your car.

As in so many areas of life, the nation thought that it was now time to reap the rewards of its hard work, and, in this case, to have a little fun. Sir Norman Birkett summed the feeling up in *National Parks and the Countryside*, written in 1945: 'After the experiences of the last six years, it is altogether praiseworthy that there should be a great stirring in men's minds, a vast quickening of man's social conscience. . . . it is at least inevitable that some compensation might be found . . . that there should be in the somewhat wistful phrase — "a better world".'

Innocent pleasures

Sir Norman believed that the creation of National Parks, to 'enhance and preserve natural beauty and to provide recreational opportunities for the public,' was essential for this better world. The government agreed, and in 1951 the first two National Parks were established, in the Lake District and the Peak District. They were an immediate success, partly because walking had long been one of Britain's favourite pastimes — the forerunner of today's Ramblers' Association had even organised a mass trespass at Kinder Scout, Derbyshire, in 1932 to fight for 'the right to roam'.

But as staff started to return to the tourist industry and factories began to build new miniature railways and fairground rides instead of tanks, a wealth of opportunities for taking innocent pleasures started to open up. Or re-open, in the case of Bekonscot *(left)*, the oldest model village in the world — even if the small boys seem less than impressed.

Llannerch, Zoo L245014

Maidstone, Zoo Park M9030

A trip to the zoo was something very special in post-war Britain. David Attenborough had not yet introduced the wildlife of the world to mass television audiences, and most children — and adults, too — were fascinated by the strange, exotic beasts on display. As a result, more and more zoos were built during the 50s and 60s: there were only 14 of them in Britain when World War II finished, but 250 by the end of the 70s.

Albert and the lion?

The animal liberation movement, of course, did not yet exist, and few people saw anything wrong in staring at bored, frustrated animals that were confined in barred cages *(above, middle)* in what was more a menagerie than anything else. It was only later that a slight uneasiness about the whole concept began to permeate the public consciousness. The zoos responded by giving their

Southport, Children's Zoo S160056

animals more freedom, and probably spoke of the importance of conservation. Even then, surely, few zookeepers — or parents, for that matter — were foolish enough to let a little girl ride on the back of an elephant, however small or docile it was, as happened at Llanerch, Clwyd *(far left)*.

Certainly, nothing of the kind ever happened at Longleat Safari Park, whose lions were first unleashed in the 1960s to spawn a million car stickers boasting: 'I've seen the lions of Longleat.'

Stubborn as a mule

Not all zoos caged their animals. The urban children who had been evacuated to the countryside during the war had been scared, mystified and fascinated in turn by farm animals. And for their younger brothers and sisters, and their sons and daughters, it was a very real thrill to see cows, sheep and goats for the first time, as in this children's farm 'zoo' *(left, middle)*.

Not all animals were as cooperative, but then donkeys rarely are *(below)*. Perhaps the boy should have used his apple as a bribe to get a ride instead of eating it himself.

Hawthorn Hill, Ruffs Orchard Donkey Stud H390303

Epsom, Derby Day E37012

If the more static pleasures of zoos were not to your taste, you could always spend a day at the races. And of all races to watch, what better than the Derby, run every year at Epsom since 1780 to identify the best horse of its generation.

Derby Day was — and still is— a wonderful social occasion for all racing aficionados, whatever their means *(above)*. The rich sipped champagne and ate lobster in boxes in the Grandstand, while those less well-off, probably on a charabanc outing from London, would mill around on the Hill, eating chips, drinking beer and investing a bob or two with Honest John, the bookie — and, by

and large, they wouldn't have swopped the Hill for the Grandstand even if you tipped them the wink about a dead cert.

Buy some specs, ref!

And, of course, there was Sunday morning football on the common *(right, below)*. There was as much pleasure to be gained from playing a part in the ritual theatre of a park game as in playing in it, as you abused opposition and referee alike.

For those less inclined to the dramatic, a games of bowls was just the thing *(right, above)*: staid, polite, and very, very British.

Farnborough, The RAE Bowling Green F9013

February 6, 1958
Seven of Manchester United's 'Busby's Babes' die in a plane crash at Munich Airport.

Tooting Bec, Common T58024

Skegness, the Boating Lake S134045

Some people like to relax through exertion; some prefer a more contemplative, peaceful recreation; and others find the best way to relieve the stresses and strains of life is simply to have a little fun, mixed for preference with a spot of courting.

And what could be more fun than recreating fairground dodgems on a boating lake *(above)*. Especially when the boys can chase girls, even though their waterman's skills are not all that they might be. As convention obliged, the girls look slightly embarrassed, but they do not seem discouraging.

The compleat angler

Water-skiing *(right)*, an opportunity to indulge a more vigorous path to relaxation, was new to post-war Britain. It had not been invented until the early 50s, simply because few civilian vessels had the speed to lift a skier out of the water. But water-skiing was such fun that it swiftly became very popular — especially

as it provided an ideal opportunity to show off the new season's swimwear. However, as with any popular activity in state-regulated Britain, there were soon calls for it to be controlled. In due course, beach zoning regulations and 'good-practice' guidelines came into force.

Fishing, however, was a different matter. It had long been the most popular participant sport in the country, and no government would be foolish enough to attempt to impose anything but the bare minimum of regulations on it.

So people — young men mainly — were free to take their ease on a sunny afternoon, lining the river *(far right)*. There might be a roach, a dace, a perch or a gudgeon, or even a bream — but that wasn't the point. As the old saying goes, 'There's a lot more to fishing than catching fish.' And even if your maggots and paste were not successful, there was warming consolation from within a thermos — or even a flask.

The folly of youth

In these days of theme parks and fantasy rides, it's easy to forget how much pleasure there was to be had in a simple picnic by the lake on a sunny day *(over)*. And as the opportunity to get a bit of a tan was as rare in post-war Britain as it is today, there was little hesitation about taking it.

The older people, of course, preferred to keep covered up while they took a stroll and tut-tutted in despair at the state of the younger generation. In their younger days, a tanned face had been a sign of a worker who toiled in the open air, rather than in a more respectable office.

The younger generation, however, stripped off at the first opportunity, and devoted itself to flirting and arranging dates at the pictures or dance hall. The girls in the foreground might have wanted to do the same, in the absence of their stern chaperone.

Poole, Water Skiing at Rockley Sands P72243

Anderby Creek, Fishing A210016

Overstone, Lakeside O104052

Southport, Peter Pan's Playground S160047

There were certainly amusement parks in post-war Britain, even if they could hardly be described as theme parks. 'Peter Pan's Playground' was part of one such in Southport, which had originally been opened in 1912 and named 'Pleasureland' in the 30s. During the war, it closed and the area was used as a parking site for aircraft, but it was refurbished in the 50s with new attractions, such as the 'House of Nonsense' and the 'Queen's Horses'.

All the fun of the fair

Children were no different in the 50s than now, though perhaps in an age without computers, videos and 24-hour television, they were more easily satisfied by unsophisticated pleasures. So, as always, they adored simple roundabout rides and swings *(right)*. And later, they could thrill to the climbs and swoops of the helter-skelter ride — it's still in operation at Pleasureland today.

There was plenty of fun to be had by the grown-ups, too, even if they were sometimes trespassing on their childrens' territory. The earnest-looking drivers of the dodgem cars *(above)* seem to be taking their pleasure with some seriousness — perhaps because their cars look venerable enough for pre-war Brooklands.

Southport, Peter Pan's Playground S160043

Pangbourne, High Street P5013

Picture the scene: the grown-ups' armchairs on either side of a blazing coal fire, mother doing her knitting and father smoking a pipe and reading the newspaper. The clock strikes, father adjusts a dial and a sonorous, upper-class voice intones 'This is Home Service of the BBC.'

Before the war, the wireless (never 'radio' in those days) was at the centre of family life. It was relied on for information — if it was on the BBC it must be true — and for amusement. Comedy catch phrases entered the language — 'Can I do you now, sir?', for example, from

ITMA — and the nation came practically to a halt during *Mrs Dale's Diary*. And on February 15, 1954, ten million listened to the 800th episode of *The Archers*.

The goggle-box

For a few years, television provided little competition. The change came in 1953, when, after much agonising by Buckingham Palace, it was announced that the Coronation would be televised. Thousands bought sets, and the 'goggle-box', as it was then known, started to become a fixture in

November 25 1952
Agatha Christie's *The Mousetrap* opens at London's Ambassador's Theatre.

The Cinema, RAF Hednesford H267038

Grt London, Barking, Longbridge Road B440014

the living room and a feature in the high street *(far left)*. At first, you could only watch BBC and its single channel, but in September 1955 ITV was launched, providing some competition. By 1959, the BBC announced that 5.5 million sets had been purchased in the previous two years, and that two-thirds of British homes had one.

Sitting in the back row
The pictures, also known as 'the flicks', continued to thrive. For people bored by the sight of a revolving potter's wheel in one of television's interminable interludes, there was always the attraction of the silver screen — though some screens were more attractive than others *(left and above)*. And there was a chance for some privacy for couples cuddling in the back row.

Cawsand and Kingsand, Path to the Beach C53036

Trelissick, King Harry Ferry T209003

A nice day out

If the pleasures of the television and wireless palled, you could always go out for the day. With tourist attractions open once more, there were plenty of sights to be seen and jaunts to be taken. A miniature railway ride, as at Pleasureland (*left*), was a reliable treat for the children, while a trip on the Ffestiniog Mountain Railway (*below*) mixed a taste of the real thing with breath-taking scenery.

Until the roads became crowded and cars became less of a novelty, it was common to 'go out for a drive' just for the sheer pleasure of it. You just let the road take you where it would, and if that meant taking a ferry it just added to the fun (*left below*). Or you spend a day at the seaside (*left above*), before returning to your car — exhausted but contented and refreshed.

Southport, Lakeside Miniature Railway S160003

Penrhyndendrath, Ffestiniog P31053

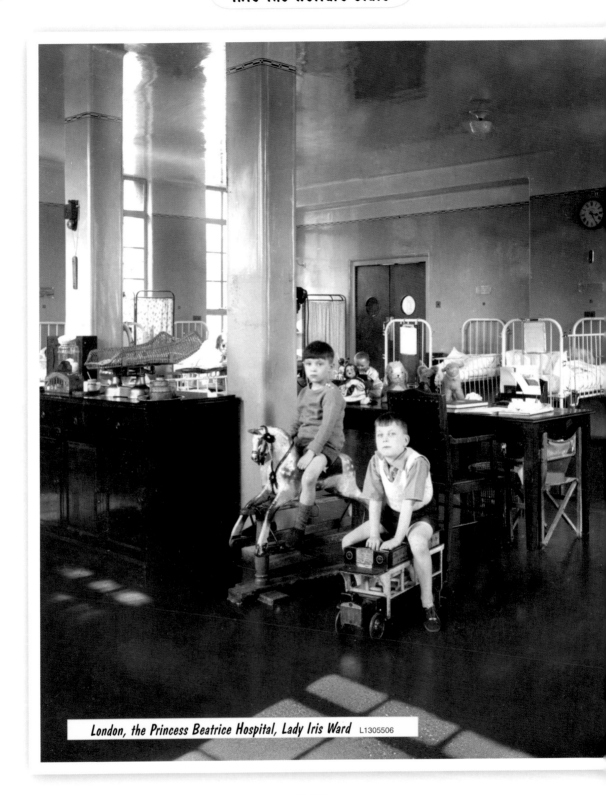

London, the Princess Beatrice Hospital, Lady Iris Ward L1305506

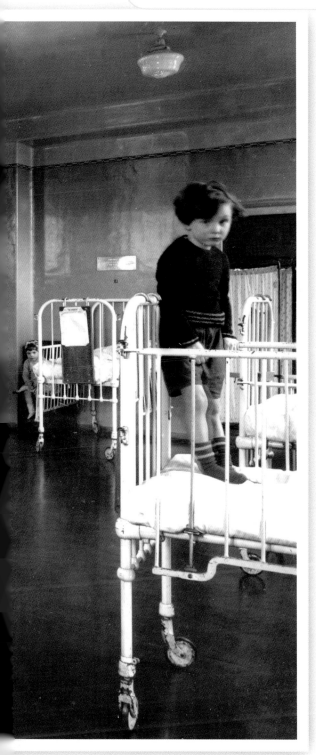

According to Sir William Beveridge, author of the 1942 Beveridge Report, there were five 'Giants' in pre-war Britain: 'want', 'sickness', 'squalor', 'ignorance', and 'idleness'. And it was essential that they were eradicated. The public certainly approved — and so, bizarrely, did Goebbels, Hitler's Minister of Propaganda, who is said to have read the Report with the greatest of interest.

'Want' was easy to define. It came from high levels of unemployment — of which 'idleness' was also a direct consequence — because unemployment assistance was only paid after a means test and only lasted for a limited period. 'Sickness' was a scourge because so many people were too poor to pay for health insurance, and even the families of people who could pay were not covered by it. 'Squalor' referred to the slum conditions endured by millions, and 'ignorance' to the fact that because fees were payable for secondary education, most children left school at 14.

Welfare versus warfare

Though important, the Beveridge Report was not revolutionary. It reflected both a long-standing body of radical thought and the general mood of a people at war, who thought that 'some good must come from it all' — the 'good' being drastic change and a move to equality. (The term 'welfare state' had been coined in the early 30s, and was often contrasted with Hitler's 'warfare state'.)

The Labour government was elected in 1945 with a firm mandate, and it was not slow to act. National Insurance, National Assistance, housing plans and the drive to full employment started almost immediately. But the changes to health provision and the education system were perhaps the most significant of all.

If the children in London's Princess Beatrice Hospital *(left)* had been born in 1920, their lives may have been very different.

London, the Princess Beatrice Hospital   L1305507

The framework for The National Health Service was laid down during the war, when hospitals were placed under central control to cope with large numbers of civilian casualties. It was predicted that 300,000 would die and 600,000 would be wounded every month, because, as ex-Prime Minister Stanley Baldwin had said in 1932, 'the bomber will always get through'.

The new organisation was called the 'Emergency Medical Services', and soon more operating theatres and wards were being built and transfusion and ambulance services were set up. Also, significantly, EMS hospitals did not charge servicemen and women. Later on, anyone involved in the war effort was also treated for free.

The EMS generally worked well, and the advantages of centralised control seemed obvious: it appeared that there was not only a moral but a practical case for a national health service, free to all at the point of delivery.

'Beveridge Day'

The Labour government created Britain's National Health Service by statute in 1946, but it did not formally come into existence until July 5, 1948. This could almost have been called 'Beveridge Day', because it also marked the passage into law of the Industrial Injuries Act and the National Assistance Act (a safety net beneath the National Insurance system).

There was much to be done in the intervening two years. The main task was to persuade a reluctant medical establishment to join the NHS, and it was handed to perhaps the most anti-establishment figure possible: Aneurin 'Nye' Bevan, the Minister of Health, a left-wing Welsh firebrand who had once been a miner.

Stuffing their throats

Bevan's tactics were simplicity itself: he bought the doctors off. As late as January 1948, doctors voted overwhelming to reject the NHS, but Bevan, in his words, 'stuffed their throats with gold.' They would be salaried, could continue to practise privately and even keep private beds in hospitals. By July 5, 90 percent had signed up to the NHS.

So brave new Britain had a brave new health service. But the budget was only £130 to £150 million a year, and with building materials in short supply it was possible only to patch up old hospitals, such as Princess Beatrice Hospital on these pages, rather than build new ones. Even so, the NHS really was at the time, the envy of the world.

London, the Princess Beatrice Hospital, Henriette Vandenbe L1305501

Wickford, the Nurses Home at Runwell Hospital W195028

The relatively modest budget for the NHS had other repercussions, too. The expectation had always been that demand would slack off as the nation became healthier. Instead, it exploded. In fewer than two years, for example, so many people had asked for false teeth and spectacles that Hugh Gaitskell, the Labour Chancellor, imposed charges on them in the April 1951 budget — predictably, Nye Bevan resigned. And in 1952, prescription charges were introduced.

A sense of security

The NHS may have strained the nation's finances almost to breaking point, but it was immensely popular: in 1953, seven out of ten people polled were very satisfied with the NHS. And the statistics are compelling: since the NHS, the infant mortality rate has dropped from 43 per 1,000 births to 9. Above all, though, it gave the nation a sense of security, from cradle to the grave, from sickness to recuperation.

Woodhouse Eaves, Charnwood Forest Children's Convalescent Home W367024

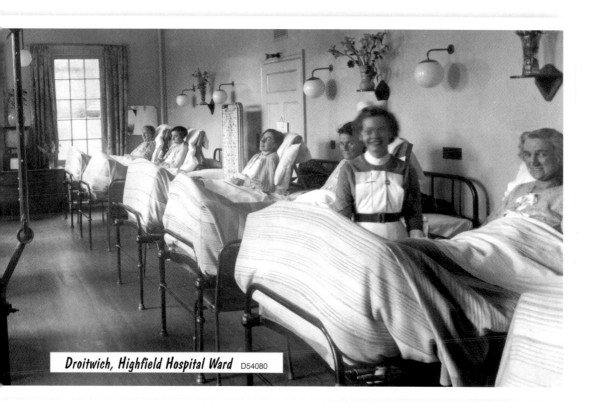

Droitwich, Highfield Hospital Ward D54080

Farnham Royal, Recuperative Home F195056

Hindhead, Dining Room, Marchants Hill H86087

Educational Reconstruction, a government White Paper of 1943 set the tone for education in post-war Britain: 'In the youth of our nation we have our greatest national asset. Even on the basis of mere expediency, we cannot afford not to develop this asset to our greatest advantage.'

Certainly Britain's youth — or at least the majority of Britain's youth — had been treated as more of an encumbrance than an asset before the war. Secondary education cost money, and only a minority of parents could afford it. Most children were forced to leave school at fourteen and look

for a job, in order to supplement their family's meagre income. The idea of going to university was little more than a dream.

Education for all

The Butler Education Act of 1944 changed all that. Now it was recognised that education led to both opportunity and status, and 'secondary education for all' became a slogan of the day. Fees in state-maintained secondary schools were abolished, and elementary schools were no more. Instead, children would attend primary school until the age

of eleven and then transfer to a secondary school. Whether this would be a grammar school or a secondary modern was decided by the dreaded eleven-plus exam; thereafter the future depended on the new General Certificate of Education exams, introduced in 1948.

Essential skills

The Butler Education Act brought about a major change in British society. By January 1955, there were more than twice the number of children still studying at school at seventeen than there had been before the war, all learning the skills that were essential if brave new Britain was to be a success. Even if the children in Marchants Hill School seem somewhat less than excited about it, the fact is that they had been given an opportunity denied to their parents.

Hindhead, Dining Room, Marchants Hill H86085

The problem for Education Minister Ellen Wilkinson was to put the theory and the plans into practice. First, there was a desperate shortage of teachers, so 35,000 of them were recruited from war service and put through an emergency training scheme. The scheme was successful but the training took time, so while the school leaving age increased to fifteen in 1945, the change could not be put into effect until 1947.

The price of learning

Then there was the problem of the infrastructure: there were simply not enough schools, and there would soon be around six million children to fit in them as the baby-boomer generation started to come through. So even though both builders and building materials were in short supply, an extraordinarily ambitious building programme was started: around 900 primary schools alone were built between 1945 and 1950.

All this came at a price, of course, and by the end of the 40s education was accounting for ten percent of the country's gross national product.

Bisley, the School B109026

Horndean, the School H403039

Mickleham, Box Hill School M69026

The village school still had its place in the scheme of things *(above, left)*, but now its capacity was augmented by new prefabricated buildings. And inside them, a strange sight for today's eyes: children sitting quietly, in serried rows of desks, facing the blackboard and learning "Reading, 'Riting and 'Rithmetic", the three Rs, with punishment awaiting any child that stepped out of line — the cane for boys and a slap on the wrist for girls.

Not that the children seemed to mind. Life in the playground went on much as before, with the girls dancing *(left)*, skipping, playing one-potato, two-potato and giggling; while the boys played marbles, conkers, jackstones and scrapped around and showed off.

It all makes the prep school boys *(above, right)*, as they seem to be, appear very constrained — but then class was still very much alive.

The demand for new schools was such that the private sector also expanded. The Victorian mansion at Woolpit *(below)*, for example, was turned into a prep school just after the war. Specialist schools were also established, such as Garston Manor *(right),* a medical rehabilitation school.

No selection

Having established the principle that education should be accessible to all, the government and educational theorists started to look more closely at the principle of selection. It was felt that failing the eleven-plus could leave a child with a life-long stigma, and that selection at such an early age was intrinsically unfair. The solution, they believed, was the comprehensive school, open to all.

The first three comprehensive schools, which were modelled on American high schools, were opened by Middlesex County Council in September 1948, in Potter's Bar and Hillingdon. It was a bold experiment, especially because each one had around 2,000 pupils. The Ministry of Education asked for a report on them, and the idea was deemed a success. London County Council came next, with three comprehensives a few years later, and then Leicestershire, Anglesey and Coventry followed the lead. By 1950 there were twenty in the country.

Harrumph!

Inevitably, comprehensive schools were not to everyone's taste. In 1956 the Headmaster of Eton said that they posed a real threat to education.

Peaslake, Woolpit School Playing Fields P16017

Garston, Manor   Games Lawn

Brave new Britain had tackled primary and secondary education, and now it was time to reform the tertiary system: the universities.

By 1951, the children whom the Education Act had first allowed to enter secondary schools were ready to go to university — and places were needed for them. At first, existing colleges were turned into universities: Hull, Leicester and Keele universities were created in this way. Later it was announced that universities would be built at Colchester, Canterbury and Coventry. And for the lucky few there were even the bastions of tradition, excellence and privilege at Oxford and Cambridge *(below)*.

August 23, 1948
The Ministry of Education calls for a report into Middlesex County Council's experiment with the new 'comprehensive' schools.

Cambridge, St John's College Tennis Court C14016

Bournemouth, the Arcade B163153

In 1961, Yorkshire housewife Viv Nicholson won a fortune on the football pools. When the newspapers asked her what she was going to do with all the money, her memorable reply was 'Spend, spend, spend!' Her answer was very much in tune with the mood of brave new Britain at the time.

It had all been so different at the end of World War II, and for about ten years afterwards. Nearly full employment meant that there was plenty of money available, but there was hardly anything to spend it on. Most of the basics were rationed, and few luxury items were in the shops.

There were a number of reasons: first, industry had to concentrate on rebuilding Britain's infrastructure; second, the country could not afford unessential imports and fund the Welfare State as well as its forces worldwide; third, the phrase 'export or die' had entered the language, in a drive to improve the balance of payments. The restrictions were all-encompassing, and often petty. All coloured pottery, for example, was reserved for the export market; only white cups and saucers were allowed to be sold in Britain.

Living off watercress

So 'austerity' was the watchword, yet Sir Stafford Cripps, the Chancellor, regularly demanded further sacrifices. Wearing a hair-shirt may have appealed to this socialist vegetarian described by Harold Macmillan as 'A strange, monastic-looking man, emaciated and said to live off watercress grown off the blotting paper on his desk,' but post-war Britain felt it deserved better.

And better times were around the corner. Import controls and credit restrictions were eased in the early 50s, then rationing was abolished and spending slowly started to rise. Soon shopping became a serious, almost intense business, as can be seen in this Bournemouth arcade scene *(left)* of the mid-50s. A nation starved of consumerism was embracing it avidly.

Grt London, Woodford Bridge, High Road W479013

St Austell, the High Street S6011

Post-war austerity made many of Britain's high streets rather sombre, gloomy places *(above, and right, below)*, with little of the hustle and bustle of earlier or later years on display. There were no groups of youths hanging around on street corners — they were either at school or at work. And in these days of full employment there were also few men of working age to be seen.

So generally the streets were left to housewives and mothers with their prams, who carried the essential item of shopping equipment at the time: a wicker basket. Sadly there was little chance for them to window shop, because there was so little on display.

Service with a smile

Apart from the shortages, though, everything was reassuringly familiar once you were inside a shop. You approached the counter, asked for the goods you wanted and then, provided you could hand over sufficient ration coupons, were served

with them — shopkeepers still prided themselves on and advertised their 'personal and efficient service'. And then a smart young boy on a bicycle would deliver your purchases to your home.

Bull's-eye

Of course a child's idea of shopping was a visit to the confectioner's. There, bull's-eyes, sherbet lemons and toffees stored in glass jars on the shelves would be poured into brass scales before being handed over in a paper bag. Sheer bliss.

Loughborough, Market Place L197010

While Britain trudged its way through drab austerity, it was boom time in America, as the first you-name-it-we've-got-it society was created. Economic expansion there had been triggered by defence spending during the Korean War, starting in 1950, and was to continue, almost without a break, for the next ten years.

The only thing that might have stopped that boom was any reluctance on the part of consumers to keep spending. But the wiles of the American advertising industry made sure that people continued to spend. In fact, they made people guilty if they didn't. Disciples of the psychoanalyst Sigmund Freud, such as Dr Ernest Dichter, who developed 'motivational research', were hired to sell products indirectly, by associating them with desirable images and lifestyles. So Marlboro cigarettes, for example, were promoted by a tattooed cowboy (he later died of cancer) with the slogan: 'A man's cigarette that women like too.' The concept worked in America, and would soon sweep Britain.

Night starvation

In fact, Britain had already been exposed to the dark arts of stealth selling. In the 30s, an advertising copywriter called Norman Cameron, who was

Egham, High Street E27053

Oakengates, Advertising O1030x

a friend of the poets Dylan Thomas, Robert Graves and WH Auden, came up with the phrase 'night starvation'.

Obviously 'night starvation' did not and does not exist. But the suggestion that it might and that children might suffer from it made a generation of parents feel guilty. Apparently the only cure was a cup of Horlick's Malted Milk, taken last thing at night, so Horlick's made a fortune. The whole business became a huge in-joke for the poets.

A pork pie for two?

Cameron's brainwave was ahead of its time, in Britain at least. Here advertising was generally much more run-of-the-mill, though the political slogan: 'HIGH COST OF LIVING is the high cost of socialism,' *(left, below)*, at least shows promise.

Hartlepool, Advertising H32080x

Gradually, insidiously, American-style advertising started to filter through to Britain. The first steps were tentative: it's hard to say that a pork pie is sexy, but is that what the line 'plenty for two' *(left, middle)* is hinting at?

Before long, the British advertising industry hit its stride, and the country was soon plastered with posters identifying products with different lifestyles and qualities. A rugged "man's man" quaffs a pint of beer, next to a more relaxed type ready to sip his Guinness *(above, middle)*. Less obviously, a slightly less rugged but clearly thoroughly decent person thoughtfully eats toast *(left)*, making it clear that Hovis is not only 'hearty', but golden-hearted. And we all went to work on an egg, didn't we?

London, Piccadilly Circus L1305194

Retail businesses were slow to take up the concepts of image and branding, remaining stolid and dependable *(far right)*. But industry soon ensured that its products were always in the public eye — and with the appropriate connotations. So Wrigley's chewing gum *(above)* was not only delicious and satisfying, but healthy, too, while Gordon's gin stood 'supreme', so must be best.

BUY BMC VEHICLES

NELSON

THE BEATLES

Grant's

F. W. WOOLWORTH & Cⁿ Lᵈ

JOIN OUR CHRISTMAS CLUB ENQUIRE NOW

Liskeard, Fore Street L53084

DISPENSING *Boots* CHEMISTS

STORES

FANCY CALLING STORK MARGARINE!

SPD

Huntingdon, Delivery Van H136019x

Dorchester, Market Day D44055

January 27, 1951
Rationing becomes worse than ever, with only 4oz of rump steak or 5oz of lamb chops per person each week.

Advertising had little part to play in outdoor markets. If, that is, you discounted the constant yells of 'Lovely apples, thruppence a pound,' or 'I'm not asking two bob, I'm not asking a shilling, it's yours for a tanner — it must be your lucky day,' as some Del Boy of the day plied his wares.

Pssst . . .
Markets were both convenient and cheap, and so were indispensable to both town and country dwellers. They tended to be much quieter affairs in the country *(above, right)* though, where both man and pig could take their ease and contemplate life, undisturbed by any hurly-burly.

But a market had other, more illicit attractions. In the days of rationing, it was a perfect place to indulge in the trivial but delightful triumphs and deceits of the black economy. Well-to-do women, or their prettiest daughters, and doyennes of working-class respectability

Headford, Market Day H435001

alike smiled winsomely and paid over the odds for a couple of sausages or a box of eggs, 'off the ration'. You could also buy some unusual country produce, legitimately. Open a cookery book of the time and you will find recipes for rook pie, for example, and nettles — they taste like spinach.

More dubiously, spivs in astrakhan collars lurked in the shadows, ready to sell you anything from petrol coupons — whether genuine or forged you would wait to discover — to nylon stockings or a wedding dress made from parachute silk.

Did you hear about . . .

Going to market was also a wonderful opportunity to meet your friends and discuss the world — in short, to gossip *(below)*. Newly pregnant women were given free orange juice in brave new Britain, but it was delivered by the milkman. So nothing could be hidden from the neighbours.

Croydon, Surrey Street C201323

Eype, Seascape Bungalets Shop Interior E54077

'Spam, spam, spam, spam,' sang the Monty Python team in December 1970. It was hardly surprising, because spam — 'a pink brick of meat encased in a gelatinous coating,' as even the US government called it — had played an unforgettable part in a wartime childhood. Over 100 million pounds of the stuff, which consisted of pork shoulder, ham and spices, was shipped to Britain during the war, to take its place on the nation's plates alongside powdered eggs and Woolton pie.

Unfortunately (though it has to be said that it still had a few devotees) spam remained a staple for some time after the war, simply because little else was available — as these depressing rows of tins and jars *(above)* testify.

'I'll have the rook pie'

Half-empty shops were commonplace in post-war Britain. At one time, rationing became even stricter after the war than during it. In January 1951, for example, in response to recurrent financial crises and a breakdown in negotiations about the importation of meat from Argentina, tuppence was sliced from the meat ration. Rump steak now cost 2s 8d a pound, and the ration was 4oz of it per person a week — or, as an alternative, you could gorge yourself on 5oz of imported lamb chops a week. Obesity was not a problem in brave new Britain. And rook pie became ever more popular.

Dancing in the streets

Things started to change during the early 50s, and finally, on July 3, 1954, housewives danced in London's Trafalgar Square and tore up their ration books as rationing came to an end.

Soon the shops started to fill up again, and austerity became a bad memory. Within a few years, housewives were once more able to revel in choice *(right, below)*. And by the end of the 50s, consumerist Britain was almost spoilt for it.

St Neots, Roper's Shop S37060

Newton, Holiday Centre N215023

July 3, 1954
All rationing ends, and housewives tear up their ration books in Trafalgar Square.

August 28 1959
A survey reveals that the average family spends £1 8s 1d a week on food.

Hixon, The Post Office H412005x

For many people, a shopping trip was about much more than just spending money: it was a way of life. In the countryside, for example, the village shop and the postal office — often, they were combined (*above*) — were focal points for the community. A young mother could cash a postal order, buy some groceries, find out what was on at the pictures (in this case, *Woman of Distinction*, a romantic comedy of 1950, starring Rosalind Russell) and catch up with all the news from the Women's Institute and Mothers' Union.

What is more, she would probably visit the shop nearly every day, because when fridges were few and far between and home freezers had hardly been heard of, food could not easily be stored. This was far from a hardship, because a network of buses linked the outlying communities.

A nice piece of cod

In the early 50s, as car ownership started to become more widespread, entrepreneurs hit on

Chilbolton, High Street C227018

the idea of taking groceries direct to the customers, and for a while there was a vogue for mobile shops. But it didn't last long, because housewives objected to the higher prices charged and missed the social life of the village shop.

One type of mobile shop did survive: the fish van. Traditionally, inland, rural Britain had little taste for fish, primarily because there had been so little opportunity to acquire it. By the time a fish hawker and his horse and cart had travelled more than a few days inland, his produce was far from tempting. But now, the fish van visited once a week, offering relatively fresh fish. You could try a nice piece of cod, haddock or skate — nothing fancy — or even, if you were lucky, a brace of gleaming, river-bright trout, no questions asked.

Help yourself

The very existence of mobile shops showed that there was a demand for better shopping facilities, though it was one that they could not satisfy, and it was clear that a revolution in shopping practices was inevitable.

As always, the change was led by America. Self-service stores had proved a huge success there, and it was not long before they started to appear in brave new Britain. The advantages for the consumer were obvious: the wider range of goods stocked gave more choice *(below)*; and volume-buying meant cheaper prices.

There were considerable advantages for the shopkeeper, too. Serving customers individually was time-consuming and labour-intensive, so fewer staff were needed. And experience proved that more goods and more choice meant more purchases — so much so that in May 1956 the government warned women 'not to be lured into overspending' by the self-service system.

But whether the village shop was self-service or not, mothers — and children practising to be mothers *(left, below)* — still congregated there to mull over the news of the day.

Poole, the Supermarket, Rockley Sands P72188

The Lizard, Serpentine Industry L62019

In 1901, according to census records, there were 1,399,000 farm workers in Britain; by 1961, the number had fallen to just 220,000. These cold statistics bear witness to a sea change in rural British society — and not just in farming, because in every rural community a huge number of jobs depended on agriculture, which drove the countryside economy.

The roll-call of tradesmen who earned their living by supplying farmers and farm-workers goes on and on. It includes, among others: black-smiths; coopers (who made casks and buckets); farriers; leatherworkers; potters; saddlers; shoe-makers; spinners; thatchers; wainwrights (who made carts); weavers; and wheelwrights. All of them suffered when agriculture went into decline, and since most market towns, if not villages, har-boured at least one representative of each trade, the whole countryside economy was affected.

Adapt or die

The results of the drift away from the land were not seen immediately, of course. It took time for people to come to terms with the harsh realities hidden beneath the go-ahead, stop-at-nothing-for-progress confidence of brave new Britain.

So while the advertising agencies developed new images for their brands, executives focussed on manufacturing and the export drive and the men in Whitehall were still generally considered 'to know what's best', the problems faced by the countryside tended to be considered secondary.

Without the income to invest in new machin-ery and, anyway, with no job opportunities for the workers it would replace, many farmers, and so their rural communities, were forced to stick to the old ways — they had no choice. Mind you, if they had had a choice, many might well have opted to cling on to the comforting traditions.

Meanwhile, the cannier craftsmen, like this potter *(left),* turned their rural crafts into art forms.

Garboldisham, Harvest Time G188029

Britain had to more or less feed itself for the first few years of World War II. German U-boats prowled the Western Approaches, taking a terrible toll of merchant ships that were carrying vital supplies, so the country's farming industry was put on a war footing, as part of the 'Home Front'.

To meet the crisis, agricultural workers were exempted from conscription into the armed forces, and their numbers were augmented by women, conscripted as 'Land Girls'. 'Dig for Victory' exhorted the posters, and farmers enjoyed more respect than ever before or since.

Hard choices

After the war, however, everything returned all too quickly to normal. The Land Girls went home, and the inexorable drift of workers away from the land and to the towns and cities in which opportunity lay continued. And farmers started to feel that they were hard done by once more.

They had a point. This was before the days of European funding and set-aside subsidies, and farmers were on their own. For most, the hard choice was between amalgamating with another farm to afford the combine harvesters and machinery that made farming economic, or struggling on in a family-based farm, trying to earn a living using the methods of the previous century.

Harvest heyday

It took much longer to bring the harvest in with just a mower, shire horses, and the sweat of men and boys *(above)* but it was infinitely more satisfying, as Laurie Lee describes lyrically in *Cider With Rosie*: 'The whirr of the mower met us across the stubble, rabbits jumped like firecrackers about the fields, and the hay smelt crisp and sweet. The farmer's men were all hard at work, raking, turning, loading. . . . The air swung with their forks and the swathes took wing and rose like eagles to the top of the wagons.'

Sometimes the corn or hay was stacked in the fields to dry, in 'stooks' or 'haycocks' *(right, above)*. How this was done varied from place to place: in Yorkshire, for example, two 'head-sheaves' would be placed on top of the stook to preserve it from the elements. Meanwhile, young girls would weave corn dollies, little knowing that they were primitive fertility symbols.

Harvest home

A farm labourer's day was not quite done when the harvest was home, because the horses, so vital to traditional farming, had to be fed and watered — as here *(below)*, in a scene that almost looks as if it were modelling for a Constable landscape.

Afterwards, though, there was the communal harvest supper, provided by the grateful farmer and enjoyed by all, with farmhouse cider to drink and all the wealth of the countryside to eat. And later, the best of the produce would be lovingly arranged, with an appropriate respect for God's intervention against the vagaries of nature, in the village church for the Harvest Festival.

Cowes, Harvest Time C173015

Ashford in the Water, the Day's Work Done A324001

One of the post-war survivals from a bygone age was the practice of taking a hop-picking 'holiday. For generations, whole extended families of Londoners — except for dad, if he was in work — had packed up at the beginning of each September and taken a 'Hop-picker Special' train to the abundant hop gardens of Kent.

Pulling the bines

For about four weeks, every family member, from toddler to grandmother, working as a family unit, would pick hops from six in the morning until four in the afternoon, when the shout came to 'Pull no more bines!' During the day, a measurer and a tallyman would make their rounds, counting the number of bushel baskets taken from each family's hop bin and noting it in the tallybook.

It could be hard, unforgiving, back-breaking work — especially when the thick, yellow hop pollen got up your nose or worked its way into a scratch. But for Londoners it was a welcome escape from the ever-present 'peas-soupers' of town, and also a way of earning that little bit extra to pay for school uniforms and other essentials.

Paddock Wood, Pressing the Hops P220016

Paddock Wood, Hop Picking P220020

Paddock Wood, Pressing the Hops P220016

Paddock Wood, Loading Hops for the Oast Houses P220018

Fairyland

Hop-picking holidays continued until the late 50s, when picking was taken over by machinery, but fond memories of those September weeks still linger on in London. Grandmothers today still recall the sheer *joie de vivre* of their trips to Kent — not so much of it during the working day, perhaps, but the evening revels were another matter.

Author Ernest Pulbrook described the scene in 1922: 'When dusk has fallen and the evening mists begin to rise the twinkling fires breaking out in lines . . . turn a Kentish valley into fairyland . . . and the children pass to and fro in the flicker like elves in a garden lit by glow-worms.' Magical.

Cenarth, Sheep Crossing the River C376034

Even in brave new Britain, livestock still had to be got to market, and sheared before the summer, too *(right, above)*. But stock-wagons could rarely cope with primitive rural roads, so farmers used tried and trusted methods to move their animals: a few drovers and a good dog to persuade them to travel the drovers' roads of antiquity.

Sink or swim
Generally, drovers' roads — tracks, really — took the shortest practical line between two points. If this meant that the sheep had to swim *(above)* so be it, though two coracles (still used on this river — the *Teifi* — to this day) are positioned to stop them from being swept away.

Then, after days on the road, and many extended stop-offs at wayside hostelries that invariably became known as 'The Drovers' Arms', the sheep would near their final destination: the market town. Everything stopped for sheep — especially in Wales — on market day *(right)*. And later, after business was done, the farmers would head for the eponymous 'Market Tavern'.

Another world
The contrast is extraordinary *(over)*. Also in the mid-50s, when the pictures of these pages were taken, there was so much traffic in some towns that white-sleeved policemen, proud in their kiosks, were needed to control it.

Coldbeck, Sheep Shearing C567031

Tregaron, Market Day T187005

Kidderminster, The Policeman K16031

For fish, at least, World War II was a blessing. In a conservation exercise that took place by unfortunate happenstance, there was little or no fishing in the North Sea between 1939 and 1945.

As a result, cod, haddock, plaice, mackerel, herring, lobsters and prawns were abundant after the war. More than 300,000 tonnes of cod alone were landed each year during the 50s — fish and chip fryers slept easy in those long-ago days —but fifty years later the figure had dropped to an imposed limit of 34,262 tonnes.

Tight lines

Fish were easily caught in brave new Britain. The country's fishermen did not need high-technology trawlers and floating fish-factories that vacuumed the deep in order to make a living — the old ways worked perfectly well. So much so, in fact, that

Porthleven, Preparing the Bait P84115

Portloe, Mending the Nets P245022

St Ives, Fish Sales S22024

they could afford to cut up perfectly saleable fish for bait for lobster pots *(far left)*, which had the potential to generate far more profit. And there was still time to spend an hour or so teasing out the tangles in the nets *(left)* before the sun sank.

Danger attracts

A fishing port was also a draw for tourists, who could buy fish from the quayside. But, perhaps more than that, there was something about the ruggedness of the fishermen and their fatalistic acceptance of the very real dangers involved in their trade that was enormously appealing.

The assembled tourists *(above)* were not just attracted by the sensual sights, smells and textures of the displayed day's catch, but by envy of the fishermen's lifestyles — so very different from those of bank managers and accounts clerks.

Ormesby, the Parish Church O45005

According to the Shire Horse Society, there were more than a million shire horses in Britain at the end of the 19th century; by the late 50s there were only a few thousand of them. Even so, a heavy horse was still a practical, easy-to-maintain alternative to expensive machinery in post-war Britain.

A noble tradition
Practicality was not the only attraction, though it was not one that could be underestimated. After all, horses were sufficiently versatile that you could plough a double farrow with a team of three horses *(above)*, or switch to a single farrow with

one horse. But more than that, shire horses had played a vital role in the country's history. Suffolk Punches, after all, were descended from William the Conqueror's chargers, while Clydesdales, and Percherons also had long and noble pedigree.

Decline and fall
So for a while these proud animals continued to make a significant contribution to British farming, helping sow seed *(right, above)*, rolling and hoeing *(right, below)*. Sadly though, the new farmers were more interested in acquiring shiny tractors, and the shire horses' days were numbered.

Milford, Farming M76058

Milford, Farming M76062

The photographs in this book have all been chosen from a single source - The Francis Frith Collection, the world-famous archive founded in 1860 by the Victorian Quaker and businessman, Francis Frith.

Although mass tourism was still in its infancy during the 1860s, during the next decade the railway network made it possible for the working man and his family to enjoy holidays and days out at locations all round the country. Francis Frith, with characteristic business acumen, foresaw that these new tourists would enjoy having souvenirs to commemorate their visits and days out. He began selling photo-souvenirs of towns and villages, of beauty spots and seaside resorts, and established a business in Reigate as a specialist publisher of topographical photographs. By 1890 Frith had created the greatest specialist photographic publishing company in the world, with over 2,000 stockists!

The ever-popular holiday postcard we know today took many years to appear, and F Frith & Co was in the vanguard of its development. By the early 1900s, postcards had become a hugely popular means of communication and sold in their millions. Frith's company took full advantage of this boom and soon became the major publisher of photographic view postcards.

Francis Frith died in 1898, but for the next seventy years the archive he created was expanded and developed by a team of photographers including his sons Claude and Eustace. By 1970 it contained over a third of a million pictures of 7,000 cities, towns and villages.

By the 1940s, the motor-car had opened up regions of the country which had once been remote and in the main unvisited by tourists. Print packets from the archive dating from this time hold photographs of the most obscure and out-of-the-way places taken from a multitude of vantage points and perspectives. These include coves, cliff formations, the tiniest hamlets, and deserted lanes, places which earlier Frith photographers would never have thought of visiting, for glass plates were expensive and heavy and cumbersome to transport. By the 1940s, however, negatives were no longer made of glass but of flexible film, which made them much lighter, much cheaper and more expendable. The Frith photographers were now able to indulge themselves a little, venturing further and further afield and taking many more photographs in their quest to keep abreast of the tourist. They added several thousand new towns and villages to the portfolio offered by the company, travelling the country in small vans. In more than one picture of provincial country towns, we can see the Frith vehicle parked in the market place – thus affirming to doubters in the office that they had actually made their visit!

The Frith photographers also acted as company salesmen, and when they visited a village or coastal resort they made it part of their job to canvas local businesses – hotels, guest houses and teashops were keen to have a professional photographer recording their buildings and visitor facilities. The Frith company printed low-cost postcards in small, manageable runs, which businesses could either sell or give away as part of their promotional literature. The archive contains hundreds of images showing hotel and guest-house bedrooms and restaurant areas that must have looked very stylish and modern at the time. Looking at them now, we can see how far fashions in furniture and furnishings have changed in the last half-century.

When buying postcards, most of us have hesitated over whether we should be buying a view of the beach, the promenade, the hotel where we are staying or a particularly picturesque local beauty spot. We are keen to show our friends and family the whole character of the area where we are staying. The 1950s were the time when the composite postcard, showing up to five different scenes, came into its own. The archive holds thousands of composite postcard artworks, usually depicting major seaside resorts or major towns. They were a simple device for showing the best of what a town had to offer visitors, and proved highly popular.

By the late 1950s colour printing had become widespread, and some postcard companies turned their entire operations over to the new medium. However, the Frith company in the main stuck to their traditional practices, and continued to offer their customers high quality black and white images of Britain as they always had done.

The 1950s are now a period of immense nostalgia for us. The Frith photographs of this era show our country before the rash of out-of-town development of the 1980s and before the relentless march of the motorways. We see towns and villages still dominated by regional building styles and materials, and with streets filled with local shops and services that visitors would not be able to find elsewhere. That world is long gone. Today's sophisticated high streets lined with the same few multi-national chainstores would be almost unrecognisable to people alive in the 1950s.

Author's acknowledgements

I can remember, I think, my father raising a glass and saying, 'Ladies and gentlemen — God Save the Queen', as my parents and their friends watched Queen Elizabeth II's Coronation on our new television set, of which he was so proud. And I can also recall — or maybe I've just been told about it so many times that I think I do — my mother's expression as I spat out a piece of the first banana that had been seen in the neighbourhood for over ten years, which she would doubtless have liked to eat herself. But I was born in 1951, so that's about the extent of my memories of brave new Britain.

For this reason, I have had to rely on other people's memories, and, in particular the research (but not, heaven forbid, the memory) of Jenny Sutcliffe, my partner, to whom much love and many thanks. I'd also like to thank a number of distinguished Breconians, listed here alphabetically, of course, rather than by age: Mike Goldstraw, Stephen Jones, Robin Naylor, Calvin Ottewell, Tony Tongue and Cathy Voisey. They all helped, and sometimes distracted me, enormously.

My main sources, however have been the following books: *'All Shook Up'* — *A Flash of the Fifties*, Joseph Connolly, Cassell, 2000; *A History of Medicine*, Dr Jenny Sutcliffe & Nancy Duin, Simon & Schuster, 1992; *Britain Speaks Out, 1937-87*, Robert J Wybrow, Macmillan, 1989; *British Science and Politics Since 1945*, Tom Wilkie, Basil Blackwell, 1991; *British Society Since 1945*, Arthur Marwick, Pelican Books, 1982; *Chronicle of the 20th Century*, Longman, 1988; *Fashions of a Decade — the 1940s*, Patricia Baker, Batsford, 1991; *Fashions of a Decade — the 1950s*, Patricia Baker, Batsford, 1991; *From Blitz to Blair*, ed. Nick Tiratsoo, Phoenix, 1997; *Somethin' Else — 50s Life and Style*, Rudloph Kenna & William Grandison, Richard Drew Publishing, 1989; *The 50s*, Peter Lewis, William Heinemann, 1978; *The Countryside Between the Wars, 1918-1940*, John S Creasey & Sadie B Ward, Batsford, 1984; *The Development of Social Welfare*, Eric Midwinter, Open University Press, 1994; *The Fifties — A Pictorial Review*, Chris Pearce, HC Blossom, 1991; *Understanding Post-war British Society*, ed. James Obelkevich and Peter Catterrall, Routledge, 1994; *Yesterday's Countryside*, Valerie Porter, David & Charles, 2000.

In particular, I must acknowledge an excellent book called *The Prefab Kid — A Postwar Childhood in Kent*, by Gregory Holyoake (SB Publications, 1998), which I recommend to you wholeheartedly.

Finally, I must thank my old friends Robin Hosie and Emma Worth, and thank Helen Vimpany for insisting that I 'get scribbling' and Shelley Tolcher for her stylish designs.

Aberyscir, Brecon, April 2002.

Frith acknowledgements

The Robert Opie Collection
Catalina swimwear (advertisement p14)

With thanks to Colin Billington (West Country Historic Omnibus & Transport Trust)
and Phil Platt (Rexquote Heritage Motor Services Ltd) for confirming the colour scheme
of the Grey Cars coach (image M14023 p32-3).